Before You Tuck Me In

Before You Tuck Me In

William L. Coleman

BETHANY HOUSE PUBLISHERS

MINNEAPOLIS, MINNESOTA 55438

A Division of Bethany Fellowship, Inc.

Photos by Dick Easterday, Gary Johnson, Fred Renich and Larry Swenson.

Unless otherwise indicated, all verses are taken from *The Living Bible*, copyright 1971 by Tyndale House Publishers, Wheaton, Ill. Used by permission.

Published by Bethany House Publishers
A Division of Bethany Fellowship, Inc.
6820 Auto Club Road, Minneapolis, Minnesota 55438

Printed in the United States of America

Library of Congress Cataloging in Publication Data

Coleman, William L.
  Before you tuck me in.

  Summary: A collection of devotions in verse, with related Bible verses, to be read aloud.
    1. Children—Prayer-books and devotions—English.
[1. Prayer books and devotions] I. Title.
BV4870.C625   1985   242'.62   85-26703
ISBN 0-87123-830-6

About the Author

BILL COLEMAN has written several bestselling devotional books for this age group (three to seven) besides his very popular family devotional books for older children and teens. His experience as a pastor, a father and a writer help to give him his special relationship with children. He and his family make their home in Aurora, Nebraska.

Also in This Series

Contents

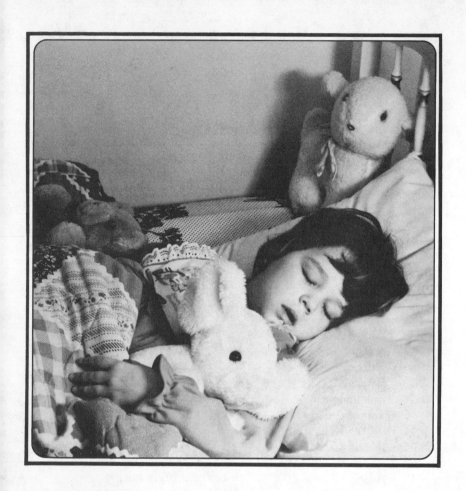

Tuck Me In

It's fun
To have someone
Cover you up,
Read to you and
Kiss you good night.

Nights are special
When someone
Who loves you
Tucks you in.

It feels good
To go to sleep
Knowing that
Everything is fine,
That your parents
Love you
And so does
God.

William L. Coleman
Aurora, Nebraska

Sleepyhead

After a good night's sleep,
It might be hard
To wake up
In the morning.

The bed feels so soft,
The covers feel so warm,
The pillow feels so fluffy.

When your parents call
To wake you up,
Or when the alarm rings
To wake you up,

You roll over
And go
Back to sleep.

If some people
Were left alone,
They would sleep all morning.

But if you sleep too much,
You are going to miss too much.

There are bikes to ride,
Forests to explore,
Boats to sail,
Houses to build,
Cookies to bake,
And other
Work to do.

People who sleep too late
Often miss out
On the good things
In life.

People who sleep too late
Often become poor
And their houses become
Rundown.

Get up
And enjoy the world
God has made.

If you sleep too much,
You may miss too much.

"If you love sleep, you will end in poverty. Stay awake, work hard, and there will be plenty to eat!" (Prov. 20:13)

A Morning Lake

When you go camping,
It's fun to sleep
Near a lake.

After you sleep
Through the night,
You wake up to see
Nature in the morning.

You might hear a robin
Calling from a tree
As you wipe the sleep
From your eyes.

Or watch a squirrel
Sneaking around
Behind the rocks.

One morning in Canada
We saw deer tracks
By the water,
And loons
On the lake.

If you stand close
To a clear lake,
You can see yourself
In the water.

The water will be
So clear and so still,
You might think
You are looking
Into a giant mirror.

As you stand
Beside the water,
It feels like God
Is standing close by.

God has created lakes
And He has promised
To lead us
Beside still waters.

After a good night's sleep
We wake up
And think about
The nearness of God.

"He maketh me to lie down in green pastures; he leadeth me beside the still waters." (Ps. 23:2, KJV)

How Do You Wake Up?

When you get out
Of bed tomorrow,
Will you be happy
Or grumpy?

Some people drag
Out of bed grumpy and
Growl at everyone.

Instead of talking
They merely grunt
And point.

Others jump out of bed
Bouncing and happy,
Eager to enjoy the day.

The grumpy people think
The happy people
Are just noisy.

The happy ones are singing,
Humming and praising God
For such a wonderful day.

The grumpy people wish
They were still in bed.

In the morning
There are grumpy children
And happy children.

And as you know,
There are grumpy parents
And happy parents.

Each of us can
Choose how he wants
To wake up.

Maybe tomorrow we will choose
To bounce out of bed,
Put on a wide smile
And thank God
For the stupendous day
He has created.

**"But as for me, I will sing each morning
about your power and mercy." (Ps. 59:16)**

Bedtime Stories

Most of us have favorite stories.
They may be about people
Or animals or about circuses.

Often we like to hear them
Over and over again.
If the stories have pictures,
We like to look at them
Before we go to sleep.

Some stories are pretend.
They are about people
Or about animals
That don't really exist.

Cinderella is a good story,
But she isn't real.
Cinderella is pretend.

Snow White and the
Seven Dwarfs is a good story.
The characters aren't real.
They are pretend.

The stories about Jesus Christ
Make good bedtime stories.
Jesus Christ is different
Than the others.
Jesus Christ is real.

Jesus Christ lived, died,
And came back from the dead.

Jesus is still alive today
And those who believe in Him
Will join Him in heaven.

Pretend stories are fun.
But so are real stories.
The stories about Jesus
Are real.

People touched Jesus
And Jesus touched them
Because Jesus is real.

"And Jesus put forth his hand, and touched him . . ." (Matt. 8:3, KJV)

Good Ears

When do you wash your ears?

Do you do it
Before you go to bed
Or do you wash them
First thing in the morning?

Do you wash the insides and
Scrub behind your ears?
If you take two mirrors,
You can see behind your ears
To see if they are clean.

Most of us use a washcloth
To clean our ears.

A giraffe can't use a washcloth,
But it can still wash its
Own ears.

This tall animal has a tongue
So long
It will reach all the way
To the giraffe's ears.

Do you ever wonder
If God has ears?
He probably doesn't have
The same kind of ears
You and I have.
But God can hear
Very clearly.

Anytime, anywhere,
God can hear us
If we want to tell
Him something.

If we want to
Ask Him for help,
Tell Him "thank you,"
Or share our feelings,
God is there.

And He hears
Very well.

"I call on you, O God, for you will answer me; give ear to me and hear my prayer." (Ps. 17:6, NIV)

Backing Off

Aren't you glad you didn't
Start shoving and pushing today?

All of us disagree
With our friends
Sometimes.

But when we see that we
Are arguing too much,
We need to back off
And stay friends.

We need to stop
When we see
Trouble coming.

If you see a coyote
Show its teeth,
If you see a skunk
Stand on its hands,
If you see a porcupine
Grind its teeth,
You know it's time to
Back off.

Smart people don't like
To fight.
It's better to be friends
With as many people
As possible.

When you begin to argue
Over a toy
Or you start yelling over
Who goes first,
You can see trouble coming.

Back off,
Give in,
Share,
Whenever
Possible.

God doesn't like
To see
His children fight.

Aren't you glad you didn't
Start shoving and pushing today?

"Don't get into needless fights."
(Prov. 3:30)

The Big Night Light

Do you like to sleep
With a night light?

Maybe you did
When you were younger,
But now
You turn it off
Before you go to sleep.

Long ago God created
A large night light
For an entire nation
Of people.

The people of Israel
Were traveling
Through the desert.

During the day
God led them
By placing a big cloud
In the sky.

At night God led Israel
With a huge flame
Shining in the air.

They knew they were safe
Because God was watching
Over them
Every night.

Every night,
Every day
God stays close
To each one of us.

Tell God
"Good night"
And have a quiet
Night's sleep.

"The Lord guided them by a pillar of cloud during the daytime, and by a pillar of fire at night. So they could travel either by day or night." (Ex. 13:21)

Riding Piggyback

Do you ever ride to bed
On your father's back?

You might climb the stairs
Or round the corner to your
Bedroom
Holding on to your father's
Back.

Families have fun doing things
Together.

Some families do not have
A mother or a father
Living with them,
But they still enjoy laughing
And climbing on each other
And rolling on the floor.

Riding piggyback
Is one of the best things
A family does.

A child can ride
High above the floor
And see all around.

He can hold on to one
Of the most important
People in his life.

Families that believe in
Jesus Christ can also

Have the added fun
Of following God together.

Whatever your family
Is like, they can
Enjoy each other.

It helps to believe in Jesus,
It helps to follow Him,
It helps to read the Bible,
It helps to worship God
As a family together.

God put families together
To love each other.

**"And the whole family was filled with joy,
because they had come to believe in God."
(Acts 16:34, NIV)**

Taking Baths

Some people can't stand
To take a bath.
Others love baths
And can spend an hour
In the tub.

Children and adults
Who like baths
Are not only
Cleaner
But are more pleasant to be
Around.

In New Guinea there is
An animal called a cuscus.
About the size of a cat,
It roams around at night
Looking for food.

A cuscus is easy for hunters
To catch.
It smells so bad
That you could find it
Even if it were hiding.

Maybe someone needs
To teach the cuscus
To take a good bath.
It might live longer.

Baths are important
For our health.
And they are important
If we want to keep
Our friends around.

In ancient Bible days
People didn't have bathtubs
In their houses.

But they still took time
To take a bath
In a nearby river.

Baths have always been
Good for people
(And animals, too).

**"A princess, one of Pharaoh's daughters,
came down to bathe in the river." (Ex. 2:5)**

Beavers and Parachutes

Sometimes animals and people
Live too close together.
People build highways and houses
And noisy racetracks.

Animals are often left
With no place to live
And nothing to eat.

In one area people
Became concerned about
The animals they were forcing
Away.

They decided to help the beavers
Find a new place to live.

Carefully they caught some beavers
And placed two in each box.
They tied small parachutes
To the boxes.

They then flew over a far-off valley
And dropped the boxes out of the plane.
Gently the parachutes floated
To the ground.

The beavers soon chewed
Through the boxes and roamed free.
They built new dams
Miles away from busy people
And loud trucks.

People need to help take care
Of animals.
That's one of the jobs
God gave to us
From the time of Adam and Eve.

Tonight there are happy beavers
Living in the open wild
Enjoying life because
Some hard-working people
Put beavers and parachutes
Together.

"God blessed them and said to them, 'Be fruitful and increase in number; fill the earth and subdue it. Rule over the fish of the sea and the birds of the air and over every living creature that moves on the ground.' " (Gen. 1:28, NIV)

Where Does Night Come From?

Why is it light
During the day
And dark at night?

Picture the earth as a ball
Spinning around.

When the place where you live
Is facing the sun,
It is daytime at your house.

But as the earth turns
Like a ball,
The place where you live
Turns away from the sun.

The half of the earth
Away from the sun
Becomes dark.
We call it night.

It takes 24 hours
For the earth to turn.
That's why it's light
Half the time
And dark half the time.

The planet Mercury
Turns so slowly its day
Lasts for almost three months.

Nighttime doesn't really
Drop like a curtain.

Night means our half
Of the earth is turned
Away from the sun.

God knew how much
Light and how much
Darkness the earth
And all of its creatures
Would need.

That's why He set
The earth spinning
Like a ball.

"He called the light 'daytime,' and the darkness 'nighttime.' Together they formed the first day." (Gen. 1:5)

A Bad Show

When Mary was little,
She watched a movie
About a forest fire.

A deer became trapped
In the fire and the show
Frightened Mary.

When she went to bed
That night she couldn't
Stop thinking
About the movie.

If children aren't careful
What they watch at night,
They can become afraid
To go to sleep.

All of us should be careful
About the things we see,
The things we hear
And the things we say
Before we go to bed.

If we think about
Good and happy things,
We will probably sleep
A lot better.

"Think about things that are pure and lovely, and dwell on the fine, good things in others. Think about all you can praise God for and be glad about." (Phil. 4:8)

The Smoke Bomb Beetle

Most of the beetles
That live on the ground
Are night creatures.

During the day
Ground beetles
Hide under rocks
Or under boards.

At night they like
To roam around
And search for food.

One of the strangest bugs
Is the *smoke bomb beetle*.
It looks harmless,
But if a bird
Tries to eat it,
The beetle drops its bomb.

The bomb is a tiny drop
Of liquid.
When it hits the ground,
The drop changes
Into a gas.

The gas
Stinks!

Any bird will turn quickly
At the smell and get away
As fast as possible.

The forest is filled
With interesting creatures
Which God has made.

Many of these creatures
Come out at night
And enjoy the world
God has made.

**"He sends the night and darkness, when all
the forest folk come out." (Ps. 104:20)**

Breathing Ice

Do you like to pretend?
Do you ever close your eyes
And picture yourself
In a faraway country?

Do you ever imagine
You are riding
On a large grey elephant
Or sailing—
Sailing across the sea?

Tonight, pretend
You can see
God breathing on
Your window.

If ice forms on
The windowpane,
Pretend it is
The breath of God.

God is close.
God is all
Around us.

We can't see Him,
But we close our eyes
And pretend we can.

Job used to do that.
He pretended that God
Breathed ice on
Rivers
And made them freeze.

We can do that, too.

As you sleep tonight,
Pretend God
Is breathing
On your window.

That's how close
God is
To each of us.

**"The breath of God produces ice, and the broad waters become frozen."
(Job 37:10, NIV)**

They Need Love

Be glad you aren't going
To marry a
White-throated wood rat.

They make terrible
Marriage partners.

White-throated wood rats
Argue all the time.
A husband and wife will
Stand on their hind legs
And fight
Like two boxers.

The two punchers don't
Live together for long.
They seem to get tired
Of fighting and soon
Go different ways.

Unfortunately their children
Grow up the same way.
They steal, fight and
Pick on other rats.

It's too bad they
Couldn't have had
A good home
Where they could have
Seen parents
Who loved each other.

Many of us are fortunate
That God has given us
Good parents
Who love each other.

Kiss your nice parents
Good night.

"Love does not demand its own way. It is not irritable or touchy." (1 Cor. 13:5)

A Lot to Think About

Do you ever lie awake
At night
Worrying about tomorrow?

Sometimes children worry
Just like their parents do.

Some children worry about
What they have to do
In school tomorrow.

Or they worry about
Going to the doctor's office.

And sometimes children worry
About things their parents
Don't even know about.

Maybe a child worries
About the money he lost.
Maybe he worries
About the big dog that
Lives down the street.

Often it helps if a child
Will tell his parents
About the thing
That worries him.
Parents like to help
When they can.

After children tell their parents
About what worries them,
They can begin to think
About God
And how much
He loves them.

Many children go to sleep
Thinking about the goodness
Of God.

They are relaxed and pleased
That God cares for them
And is with them each day
And each night.

There are many scary things
To think about
If we want to.

There are also many good things,
Like the love of God.

**"But they delight in doing everything God
wants them to, and day and night are
always meditating on his laws and thinking
about ways to follow him more closely."
(Ps. 1:2)**

If Birds Could Talk

If birds could talk,
They would have some
Great stories to tell.

They could tell us
About wild bears
They have seen.

They might tell us
About gold coins
They have seen lying
In far-off riverbeds.

Maybe they would
Tell us what
It feels like
Flying high in the air.

Of course birds can talk.
They simply don't speak
Our language.

The mockingbird not only
Can talk, but it can
Make a noise like a hawk.

Mockingbirds like to talk
At night.
Maybe while you are
In bed tonight
You will think you hear a hawk.

And it will be
A mockingbird pretending
To be a hawk.

If birds could speak
Our language
They might also tell us
About God.

Birds have seen
Many of the wonders
God has made
In nature.

Maybe they would like
To tell us
How wonderful
Our God is.

"Who doesn't know that the Lord does things like that? Ask the dumbest beast—he knows that it is so; ask the birds—they will tell you; or let the earth teach you, or the fish of the sea." (Job 12:7–9)

Angels Watching Us

We aren't sure
What angels look like.
Maybe they can change
Their appearance.

Some may have wings
And other angels
May not.

The Bible tells many stories
About angels.
They have helped people
For thousands of years.

Helping people
Is one of the main jobs
Of some angels.

Angels might keep some sicknesses
Away.
Angels might whisper to us when
We are about to do something bad.

We don't understand
All the ways
Angels help us, but they do.

You might be glad to know
That angels work
During the night.

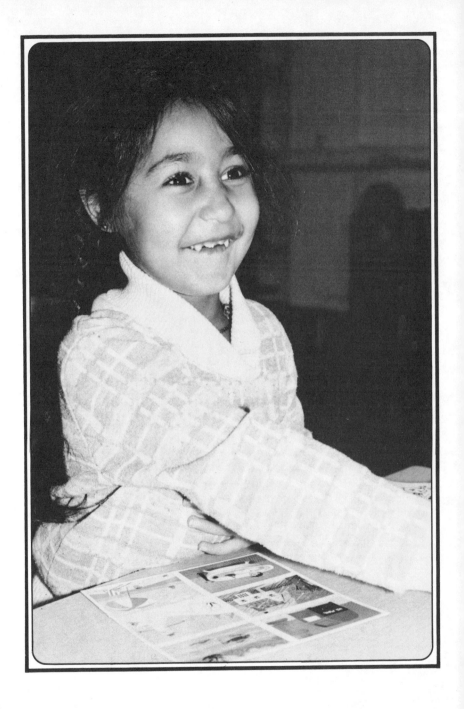

One night an angel
Helped Peter
Escape from prison.

While you are sleeping tonight,
Some of the angels will stay
Awake.

They will carry out the business
Of watching over and
Helping children like you.

Wave good night to the angels.
They will stay awake while
You are sleeping.

"The angels are . . . spirit-messengers sent out to help and care for those who are to receive his salvation." (Heb. 1:14)

A Good Father

The ostrich is a
Funny looking bird.
It is tall and
Its head reaches
Eight feet off the ground.

An ostrich is heavy.
A father might weigh
Three hundred pounds.

Ostrich eggs are so large
That one egg would be
Breakfast for three families.

The eggshell is extra thick.
It is almost as tough
As a coffee cup.

After an ostrich lays an egg,
About 40 days go by
Before the egg hatches.

Every day the mother
Sits on the egg and
Every night the father
Sits on it.

The father doesn't leave
The egg like many animals would.
An ostrich is fortunate
To have a father that cares
And stays around to help.

We can thank God
If we have good fathers
Who care about us
And are around to help.

Life goes better
When fathers and their
Children
Love each other.

"And this is the promise: that if you honor your father and mother, yours will be a long life, full of blessing." (Eph. 6:3)

Better Teeth

Have you heard the good news?
Fewer and fewer people have
Bad teeth.

Most of us are taking
Better care of our teeth.

Plus
Fluoride in our water
Makes it harder for our teeth
To decay.

Plus
Dentists now use
A chemical which is brushed
On teeth
And puts a coat on
Teeth.

That invisible coat
Makes it hard for a cavity
To start.

Some dentists believe most
Children
Will soon stop getting tooth
Cavities.

Today many children have
Already stopped getting
Cavities.

Brushing our teeth before
We go to bed
Becomes more important
All the time.

Each of us wants
Healthy,
Beautiful
Teeth.

"Your teeth are white as sheep's wool, newly shorn and washed; perfectly matched, without one missing." (Song of Sol. 4:2)

The Sun Takes a Nap

Not very often,
But once in a while,
The sun seems to go away
During the daytime.

Just like it was
Taking time off
For a nap.

It doesn't happen often
But sometimes
The moon gets
Between the sun
And the earth.

And for a few minutes
We can't see the sun
Because it is hiding
Behind the moon
During the daytime.

When the moon
Hides the sun,
We call it an eclipse.

The moon blots out the sun for
A few minutes and
Then we see the sun again.

When the moon
Is in front of the sun,
We can pretend
The sun is taking
A nap.

Most of the time
We see the sun,
And it is a special sign
That God created everything.

The sun reminds us
About God,
Except when it
Takes a nap.

"Praise him, sun and moon, and all you twinkling stars." (Ps. 148:3)

Looking for Animals

If you want to see animals,
There are millions around.
Most animals are afraid of people.
And they are hard to find.

Many hide in the grass
And may be only a few feet
Away.

Some, like the fox, are
Sly and intelligent.
They are good hiders.

Some rabbits are hard
To see
Because they roam around
At early dawn or late dusk.

If you want to see
An opossum or an owl,
You probably will have to
Stay up late at night
To find them.

Animals are all around
And can be seen
If we take the trouble
To search for them.

God is much the same
Way.
He is all around us if
We
Are willing to look for
Him.

The best place to find
God
And His only Son,
Jesus,
Is in the Bible.

If we search the Bible,
We will know
What Jesus is like,
And
We will know how
To follow Him.

"You search the Scriptures, for you believe they give you eternal life. And the Scriptures point to me." (John 5:39)

Cleaning Up

While you sleep tonight,
Nature's cleanup crews
Will be out
Keeping our world neat.

One group is called
The black burying beetles.
Their job is to remove
Dead birds or mice
Or other small animals.

The black burying beetles
Do not usually
Drag the body away
And hide it.

They begin to dig
Underneath the body
Until it sinks.
The beetles then cover it
With the earth they removed.

Black burying beetles
Love to find these bodies.
They slowly eat them
And plant their eggs
In them.

This might not sound
Great to you,
But the beetles
Enjoy it.

When the beetles
Do this
They not only
Clean up the earth,
But they also provide fertilizer
To help the grass
Grow.

God tells us
He cleans our hearts
The same way.

When we do something wrong,
We tell God about it,
And God wipes away the wrong
We have done.

God loves us,
Forgives us,
And cleanses our hearts.

That's why we tell God
When we think
We have done something
Wrong.

God can make us
Clean again.

**"Oh, wash me, cleanse me from this guilt.
Let me be pure again." (Ps. 51:2)**

Lump in Your Throat

Have you ever
Gone to bed
With a lump
In your throat?

Maybe you were sad
Because you had lost
Your favorite ring.

Maybe you felt bad
Because your parents
Had to spank you.

It feels terrible
To go to bed
With a lump
In your throat.

But often when you
Wake up in the morning,
The lump is gone.

You aren't sad
Anymore,
And you can
Smile and laugh
Again.

Sometime when you
Feel bad
At bedtime,
Ask God to take
The sadness away
While you
Are sleeping.

Most of the time
You will wake up
With a smile
On your face.

Lumps in your throat
Usually don't last.

**"Weeping may go on all night, but in the
morning there is joy." (Ps. 30:5)**

Nighttime Snacks

While you are
Tightly snuggled in bed,
The earthworm pokes
Out of its home
And goes looking for
A nighttime snack.

It doesn't eat cookies
Or leftover pizza.

An earthworm would rather
Snack on cut grass,
A few old vegetables,
Or maybe an old leaf.

If it gets lucky,
An earthworm
Might find a dead insect.

It will drag the
Insect to its home
(called a burrow)
And pull it inside.

The earthworm will then
Feed on the dead insect
For some time to come.

An earthworm likes
Its dinner best,
Mixed with a little soil.

In the morning
Most earthworms
Are safely underground
After their search
For food.

Did you have plenty
Of food today?

God is good to people
And to animals
And provides food
For them.

God also uses us
To send food
To people who are hungry.

Thank God that
You have plenty
Of food tonight.

**"He gives food to every living thing, for his
lovingkindness continues forever."
(Ps. 136:25)**

Sing Yourself to Sleep

After everyone
Has gone to bed
And you are lying
In your bed
Waiting to fall asleep,
Do you sometimes
Sing to yourself?

Maybe you hum
For a while,
Or maybe you
Sing the words, too.

After you sing
Quietly
For a while,
You start to
Get sleepy,
And your eyes
Begin to close
And then
You are
Asleep.

Some nights
You like to
Sing about God
Or the love
Of Jesus Christ.

When you sing
Softly about
The love of Jesus Christ,
It usually
Makes you smile.

And you can
Go to sleep
With a smile
On your face.

God gives us songs
Because He is
Glad
We belong to Him.

"Yet day by day the Lord also pours out his steadfast love upon me, and through the night I sing his songs and pray to God who gives me life." (Ps. 42:8)

The Deep Sleep

When winter starts coming,
Some animals get ready
For the deep sleep.

Their sleep is so deep
It is called hibernating.
This sleep can last
For as long as five months.

Woodchucks, prairie dogs
And turtles are
Some of the creatures
That hibernate.

This sleep is so deep,
The animal almost
Turns its body off.

Some animals that
Breathe 100 times a minute
The rest of the year
May reduce their breathing
To four breaths a minute.

If the heart beats 250
Times a minute,
It might slow to 10
Beats a minute.

While they sleep,
They live off
Food they ate
Just before they
Hibernated.

After working hard
To collect food
For the winter,
It must feel good
To fall into
A deep sleep.

Sleep must feel good
To you
After you have played hard
All day
Or
You have worked hard
Cleaning,
Picking up
Or
Helping.

You have had
A busy day.
Now
You can have
A deep sleep
All night.

"The man who works hard sleeps well."
(Eccles. 5:12)

A Night Light

When it gets dark
At night,
Not everything
Is dark.

Nature is alive
With the light
That God has
Created.

Some of God's lights
Live in the sea.

The round, stringy-looking
Jellyfish often has
Its own night light.

Jellyfish are also called
Sea nettles
Because they can sting
Like the needles
On a nettle plant.

At night the jellyfish
Lights up
But scientists aren't sure
Why.

Maybe it is trying
To get food to come close.

Whatever the reason,
A jellyfish never
Lives in total darkness.

At night it carries
Its own night light.

The Bible
Is like a light
In a dark world.

It helps us
See
How God wants us
To live.

The Bible is like
A night light
So we can
Follow Jesus Christ
All the time.

"You will do well to pay close attention to everything they have written, for, like lights shining into dark corners, their words help us to understand many things that otherwise would be dark and difficult." (2 Pet. 1:19)

Under the Covers

How do you like to sleep?
Do you keep your head
Above the covers
Or do you pull the covers up
Over your head?

Maybe you pull the covers up
Just over your nose
So you can still see
Around the room.

Maybe you sleep
On your side
And pull your covers up
Over one ear.

People often do
Strange things
With their covers.

The red fox
Also has a cover.
It carries it everywhere.

When a red fox
Takes a quick afternoon nap
Or a long sleep,
It curls up
Into a ball
And covers
Part of its face
With its tail.

The tail
Helps keep its face
And paws
Warm
While it sleeps.

You can't feel it,
But God puts
His cover over you.

You can't see it,
But God
Pulls a cover over you
As you sleep.

When God says
He watches over you,
It is just like
God is pulling
His cover up
To keep you
Warm and comfortable.

You can almost feel
God pulling up His covers
Over you
Tonight
As He
Tucks you in.

**"The beloved of the Lord shall dwell in
safety by him, and the Lord shall cover him
all the day long, and he shall dwell between
his shoulders." (Deut. 33:12, KJV)**

The Animal with a Camper

If you were a
Chilean flamingo,
You could sleep
Without using a bed.

When this flamingo
Gets tired,
It simply lifts
One leg
And stands steady
On the other leg.

Then the flamingo
Tucks its head
Underneath its wing.

The flamingo goes to sleep
Standing on one foot.
It is like carrying
A camper
On one's back.

It must be quiet
And dark
And warm
And cozy
Under a flamingo's
Wing.

The flamingo
Doesn't seem to care
If it is standing

In some water
Or standing
On land.

Tonight
When you are tucked in,
And quietly fall asleep,
It will be just
As if
You were sleeping
Underneath
The wings of God.

He will draw you
Close to himself
And hold you
And love you.

Pretend that
You can see
God's wings
Over you
Protecting you
All night
Long.

**"How much you have helped me—and how
I rejoice through the night beneath the
protecting shadow of your wings."
(Ps. 63:7)**

Twinkling Stars

Why do some stars
Twinkle
While other stars
Shine steadily?

The ones that twinkle
Make the sky more interesting,
Like a Christmas tree.

Stars look like they twinkle,
But they really don't.

We see through the air,
And sometimes the air is
Moving.

Moving air makes
A star look like
It is twinkling.

Twinkling adds
Beauty to the world
God has made.

A twinkling star acts
Like an electric sign.
The twinkling stars remind us
There is a God.

This sign in the sky
Tells us to remember God.
God is greater than the stars.
And yet God is closer
Than your hand.

When we look at
The twinkling stars
We remember how
Powerful, great, loving
And caring
Our God is.

It's good to have
Twinkling stars
To remind us about God.

"Praise him, sun and moon, and all you twinkling stars." (Ps. 148:3)

The Animal Motel

The greater rhea
Is a large bird
That cannot fly.

It lives in South America,
Mostly in Brazil and Argentina.

Greater rheas make
Excellent fathers.

If something gets near
His chicks,
The greater rhea
Attacks.

He will
Chase animals away
And has been known
To attack people
And small airplanes.

At night
He becomes very peaceful.

He likes to kneel down
And become a motel
For his baby chicks.

Some of the chicks
Will crawl underneath
The father.

They like
The lower rooms.

Other chicks will climb
Up on the father's back
And look for places
To sleep
Under his wings.

If it rains at night,
The chicks are safe
And dry
In the animal motel.

Jesus wants us
To come to Him
Just as chicks
Come to a
Greater rhea.

We can live
With Jesus Christ
Every day
And forever.

Like a giant bird,
Jesus welcomes us
As if we
Were living
Under His wings.

There is enough room
In Jesus
For everyone.

**"How often I have wanted to gather your
children together as a hen gathers her
chicks beneath her wings." (Matt. 23:37)**

Darkness Is Our Friend

Some children are afraid
Of the dark.
Even some adults
Have to sleep
With a light on.

Most of us
Learn
That the darkness
Can't hurt us.

Darkness is our friend.
It lets us sleep
Without light
Shining in our eyes.

Darkness is our friend.
It stops us from
Seeing things around us
So we have fewer things
To think about.

Darkness is our friend.
It helps us talk less
And slows us down
So we can sleep.

Some children are afraid
Of the dark
Because they think darkness
Is bad.

The darkness in our bedroom
Is our friend.
It allows us to slow down,
It allows us to rest,
It allows us to go
To sleep.

Let the darkness
Be your friend
Tonight.

Turn the lights out.

**"Now you don't need to be afraid of the
dark any more." (Ps. 91:5)**

Tossing and Turning

Have you ever watched
A row of birds
Standing together
Trying to sleep?

On a cold night
They move around
A lot.

The birds on the ends
Get most of the
Cold breezes.

When the bird
On the end
Gets tired of shivering,
It will hop
Into the middle
And push for a place
To stand.

Soon the bird
At the other end
Will hop into the middle, too.

Each bird
Wants to keep warm.

People often
Toss and turn
In the night
Trying to get
To sleep,
Too.

We fluff up
Our pillow
Or pull
At our covers.

But other nights
We go to sleep
Right away
And sleep soundly.

We sleep quietly
And God gives us
The peace to be calm.

**"Peace be to all of you who are in Christ."
(1 Pet. 5:14)**

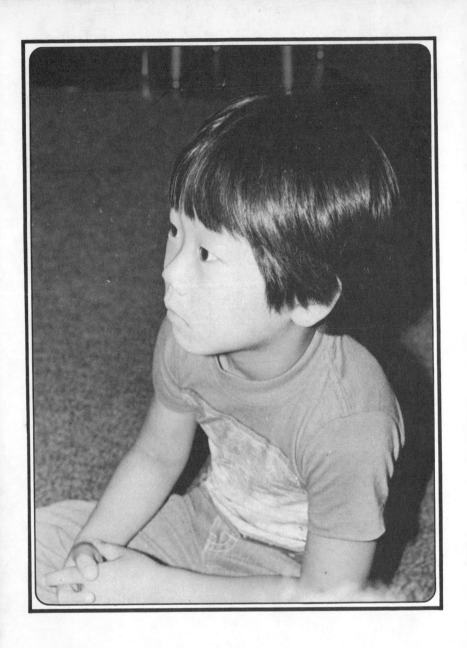

Why Do People Snore?

If you listen to some people
As they are sleeping,
You will hear
Strange noises.

Many people snore
In their sleep.
Maybe you are
A good snorer.

Children don't seem
To snore as well
As mothers and fathers.

People who breathe
Through their mouths
Are more likely
To snore.

Your mouth has
A soft place
On its roof.

As air moves across
The roof of your mouth,
It makes a noise.
That's the noise we call
Snoring.

When your mouth dries,
The noise might get louder.

Your lips, cheeks and mouth
May also start to move
As the air travels
In and out.

Mouths are able to make
All sorts of strange noises.

A mouth can also make
Beautiful sounds.
It can even praise God
By saying
How great and wonderful
He is.

God creates mouths
To say wonderful things.

"My mouth shall praise thee with joyful lips." (Ps. 63:5, KJV)

Who Planted the Yucca?

Tonight the yucca plant
Will open and bloom.
It will give off
A beautiful scent
To go with its white color.

The bright color and good smell
Help bring the female yucca moth.

The Indians had many uses
For the yucca plant.

From this plant they made
Rope, shoes, baskets and mats.
The Indians ate the buds,
Sometimes without cooking them.
They even made a drink from
The plant.

Indians used every part
Of the yucca.
They turned the stems and roots
Into soap.
Some called it the soapweed.

Where did the yucca plant
Come from?
Maybe it was planted
In the first garden.

The first garden ever
Was planted by God.

After God planted the garden,
He put Adam in it
As the first gardener.

Maybe the first garden
Had a yucca plant
Planted by God.

**"Then the Lord God planted a garden in
Eden, to the east, and placed in the garden
the man he had formed." (Gen. 2:8)**

Night Anchor

When we went sailing
In Washington state,
We decided to sleep
In the sailboat.

To stop the boat
From floating out to sea
At night,
We dropped an anchor.

The anchor was
A piece of metal
Tied to a rope.
It kept the boat
From moving.

When we woke up
In the morning,
The boat was
In the same place
As when we went
To sleep.

An anchor keeps
Us in the same place.

Jesus is like
An anchor.

He keeps us
Close to God
While we are asleep.

And while we
Are awake.

You can sleep tonight.
The Jesus anchor will
Keep you close to God.

"We have this hope as an anchor for the soul, firm and secure." (Heb. 6:19, NIV)

The Miserable Mink

How could anything
Be as pretty as a mink
And still be so ugly?

A mink has beautiful fur,
But it is so mean
It has trouble getting along
With another mink.

Tonight while you are sleeping,
The United States and Canada
Have mink running all over.

They are looking for eggs, small birds,
Fish or frogs for their supper.
Their long bodies twist easily
So they can squeeze through fences
Or tiny holes.

Many mink seem grumpy and miserable
Most of the time.
They would rather fight animals
Than try to get along.

Just because someone is pretty
On the outside
Doesn't mean he is pretty
On the inside.

If we are grumpy and
Always want to argue,
We act ugly
Even though we
Look pretty.

The Bible tells us
To be friendly
And kind.

We can try to
Live at peace
With everyone.

**"Don't quarrel with anyone. Be at peace
with everyone, just as much as possible."
(Rom. 12:18)**

The Fingers of God

You probably have
A good imagination.
If you were asked
To describe what was in
A treasure chest,
You could tell about
Gold necklaces
And silver bracelets
And strings of pearls.

As you lie in bed tonight,
Move your fingers
Through the air
And imagine—
Imagine they are
The fingers of God.

Picture yourself
Holding the earth
On your fingertips.

Use your hand
To separate
The darkness
From the light.

Gently toss the stars
Into space
And place the sun
In the sky.

Don't forget to stick
The moon in its place
To watch over the night.

When you put the
World together, remember
How God created it
All.

The God who put
Each star in place
Is the same God
Who loves you tonight.

Thank Him
For watching over you.

Tell God
Good night.
You need to go
To sleep.

**"When I consider your heavens, the work of
your fingers, the moon and the stars which
you have set in place. . . ." (Ps. 8:3, NIV)**

Dreaming in Color

Probably all of us dream,
And we dream often.

However, when we wake up
We have trouble
Remembering our dreams.

Scientists believe most of us
Dream in color.
But a few people stick
To black and white.

Dreams affect our bodies.
If we dream about running
To catch a train,
Our heart will beat faster.

Often our eyes will move
Under our closed eyelids.
We might be watching our dream
As we would a television show.

Some of us have frightening dreams
After we hear or see a scary story.
Many people stay away
From scary stories,
Especially close to bedtime.

God doesn't want us to spend
The night
Worrying over a frightening dream.

He would rather see us have
A good night's sleep
So we can have a better
Tomorrow.

"God wants his loved ones to get their proper rest." (Ps. 127:2)

Close Your Ears

Have you ever tried
To go to sleep
But couldn't
Because of the noise?

Sometimes you wish
You could close your ears
And shut off
All the noise.

The American opossum
Can do just that.

It can fold
Its long ears over
And shut out
The noise.

It doesn't need
Covers or pillows
To keep out
The noise.

Its long ears
Do the job.

Sometimes it's nice
To lie awake
In the quiet night
And think about
God
And all that
He
Does for us.

We turn off
The radio
And everyone stops
Talking and
We can think about
God.

The quiet night
Is a good time.

**"Be silent, all mankind, before the Lord."
(Zech. 2:13)**

Before You Sleep

Before you go to sleep
Tonight,
Before you close your
Eyes,
And drift off in peace,

You might want
To tell Jesus Christ
That you love Him,
That you trust Him,
That you want Him
In your life.

Jesus wants to be
Part of your life
Tonight,
Tomorrow
And
Forever.

Jesus wants to be
Your friend,
Your Savior
And
Your Lord.

But Jesus wants
To be asked
To be part
Of your life.

Tonight would be
A good time
To ask Jesus
To come into
Your heart and life.

Tonight
You might want
To tell Jesus Christ
That you love Him,
That you trust Him,
That you want Him
In your life.

**"If you believe that Jesus is the Christ—
that he is God's Son and your Savior—then
you are a child of God." (1 John 5:1)**

Fireworks

On a clear night
You might see a ball of fire
Shooting through the sky.

We often call this a
"Shooting star."
It's all right
To call it that,
But it isn't really a star.

The balls of fire are really
Pieces of stone or metal
That have broken loose.

As they come racing
Toward the earth,
They become hot
And begin to burn.
We might see their fire
As white or yellow
Or red or even green.

Sometimes they fall through
The sky in bunches.
We call that a "meteor shower."

Most of these fireballs burn up
Before they hit the earth.

"Shooting stars" are fairly harmless,
But they are beautiful to watch.

They travel through the sky
Like God's fireworks.

If we want to, we can
Think about God
When we see them.

They can remind us
That God has created
A beautiful universe,
And we can praise God
For all He has done.

"Praise him, skies above." (Ps. 148:4)

Big-eyed Bushbabies

If you lived in South Africa,
You might see two yellow eyes
Hiding in the bushes
During the night.

The animal is called a bushbaby.
It likes to sleep all day
And play at night.

Bushbabies are cute.
They look like they are
Part cat, part mouse,
Part squirrel, and they have
Back legs like a kangaroo.

Their favorite way of moving around
Is to jump.
Instead of walking or running,
They leap everywhere.

They spend
Part of their nights
Looking for insects for food.
But they don't work
All the time.
Bushbabies enjoy playing.

You probably wouldn't see
A bushbaby at night
Because they hide so well.

But their shining eyes
Give them away.

You might look into
A tree or a bush
And see two eyes
Looking back at you.

Their eyes see in the dark
A little like God's eyes
See us.

Whether we are playing
Or walking
Or sleeping,
God can see us
Through the darkness.

God looks at us
With love
And care
Even though we
Can't see Him.

"For the eyes of the Lord are intently watching all who live good lives." (Ps. 34:15)

Humming to Sleep

Singing at bedtime
Is sometimes too noisy.
Instead of helping you
Go to sleep,
Singing can keep
You awake.

Maybe tonight you
Would enjoy humming
Yourself to sleep.

Do you know
Some songs about God
That you could hum?

Would you like to
Make up some songs
Of your own?

You could hum songs
About God
That you made up.

It would make you
Feel good
To go to sleep
Humming songs about God
That you made up.

Best of all,
God would enjoy
Listening to them.

**"Sing to the Lord, for he has done
wonderful things." (Isa. 12:5)**

Signs in the Sky

Not far from our house
A restaurant
Sells hamburgers
And ice cream.

The restaurant has a large sign
With bright lights.
The lighted sign tells people,
"This is a restaurant!"

At night people can see
The sign
From many blocks away.

God wants to tell people
About himself,
So He has put signs
In the sky.

On many nights
We can see God's signs.

One of the reasons
God put stars in the sky
Was to give people
Lighted signs.

When we look at the stars,
We often think about God
And His tremendous ability.

God created billions of stars.
We can't see all of them.
But the stars we can see
Are signs to tell us
About God
In the night.

When most people
Have gone to bed,
The signs keep shining
In the sky.

Before you go to sleep
Tonight,
Look outside for God's
Lighted signs.

"Praise the Lord, O heavens! Praise him from the skies!" (Ps. 148:1)

Never Sleep on a Windowsill

The Bible tells us
About a young man
Who was sitting
On a windowsill
Listening to a sermon.

The sermon got long
And it became very late
At night.

Though he tried to stay awake,
The young man kept dozing off.
He fought to keep his eyes open,
But it was too hard.

Finally the man went to sleep
And fell out of the window.
K-ER-PLUNK!

Windowsills make
Miserable beds.

It's safer to find
A soft bed
Or a couch
Or even a warm floor
Before you go to sleep.

Who wants to go to sleep
And go
K-ER-PLUNK?

**"A young man named Eutychus, sitting on
the window sill, went fast asleep."
(Acts 20:9)**

Sweet Breath

Before you go to sleep
Tonight,
You could do your teeth
A favor.

Tell your teeth good night.

To make sure they have
A good night,
You will want
To brush them.

When we forget to brush
Our teeth,
Tiny pieces of food
Begin to decay or rot.

The rotting food between
Teeth
Begins to stink.

When you wake up
Tomorrow,
Your breath could smell
Bad
Because of the
Rotting food
Inside your mouth.

Did you brush
Your teeth
Before you came to bed?

If you did,
You will
Wake up tomorrow
With breath
That smells sweet
And pleasant.

". . . and the scent of your breath like apples. . . ." (Song of Sol. 7:8)

The Buzzing Mosquito

Have you ever been lying
In bed
Ready to fall asleep
When
You heard the noise
Of a mosquito
Flying around your ear?

A mosquito's buzz
Is an unpleasant sound
Because you think
It is going
To bite you.

You slap at the mosquito
In the dark
Hoping to hit it
Because you don't want
To be bitten.

Why would God make
Pests like mosquitoes?
Does He create things
Just so they can bite
Us?

Mosquitoes have
A good purpose.
Animals like frogs and fish
Eat mosquitoes.
We in turn eat fish
And some people eat frogs.

God created mosquitoes
For a purpose.
They were made to be
Eaten.

We just wish
The frogs and fish
Would eat more
Of them.

"For everything God made is good."
(1 Tim. 4:4)

In a Sinking Ship

Where is the strangest place
You have ever gone to sleep?

Have you ever been
To a noisy baseball game
With hundreds of people
Shouting and screaming?

If you looked around
You could probably see
A child
On his father's lap
Fast asleep.

The noise didn't wake
Him up because
It feels so good
To sleep.

There was a terrible earthquake
In California,
But one lady said she
Didn't hear a thing.

She slept right through it.

Sleep is one of God's
Greatest gifts.
It feels great to get
A good night's sleep.

Jonah was one of
The world's best sleepers.

He was on a ship
When a huge storm
Came up.

Everyone on the ship
Became frightened
And began running
Around.

They screamed
And threw things
Overboard.

But Jonah was snuggled up
Inside the ship
Asleep like a baby.

Sleep is one of God's
Greatest gifts.

**"Fearing for their lives, the desperate
sailors shouted to their gods for help and
threw the cargo overboard to lighten the
ship. And all this time Jonah was sound
asleep down in the hold." (Jonah 1:5)**

Elephant Hugs

If you are as big
As an elephant,
You have to be careful
Whom you hug.

It's even hard
For an elephant
To hug another elephant.

But elephants need each other
And they like each other.
So sometimes they enjoy
Hugging each other gently.

Two elephants
Might touch trunks
Or rub foreheads.
At other times
They rub their tusks
Against another's tusks.

A tusk rub can be a
Big deal.
Some elephant tusks weigh
Over 400 pounds each.

People are a little bit
Like animals.
We like to be touched
And held
By our parents.

Before you go to sleep
Tonight,
Give your parents
A big, firm hug.

It tells them
You love them.

When Jesus prayed for children,
He would put His hands
On them
Because He loved them.

It feels good
To hold someone
You know and love.

"And he put his hands on their heads and blessed them before he left." (Matt. 19:15)